Night Flight

Level 4 – Blue

Helpful Hints for Reading at Home

The graphemes (written letters) and phonemes (units of sound) used throughout this series are aligned with Letters and Sounds. This offers a consistent approach to learning, whether reading at home or in the classroom.

HERE IS A LIST OF PHONEMES FOR THIS PHASE OF LEARNING. AN EXAMPLE OF THE PRONUNCIATION CAN BE FOUND IN BRACKETS.

Phase 3			
j (jug)	v (van)	w (wet)	x (fox)
y (yellow)	z (zoo)	zz (buzz)	qu (quick)
ch (chip)	sh (shop)	th (thin/then)	ng (ring)
ai (rain)	ee (feet)	igh (night)	oa (boat)
oo (boot/look)	ar (farm)	or (for)	ur (hurt)
ow (cow)	oi (coin)	ear (dear)	air (fair)
ure (sure)	er (corner)		

HERE ARE SOME WORDS WHICH YOUR CHILD MAY FIND TRICKY.

Phase 3 Tricky Words			
he	you	she	they
we	all	me	are
be	my	was	her

Phase 4 Tricky Words			
said	were	have	there
like	little	so	one
do	when	some	out
come	what		

TOP TIPS FOR HELPING YOUR CHILD TO READ:

• Allow children time to break down unfamiliar words into units of sound and then encourage children to string these sounds together to create the word.

• Encourage your child to point out any focus phonics when they are used.

• Read through the book more than once to grow confidence.

• Ask simple questions about the text to assess understanding.

• Encourage children to use illustrations as prompts.

This book focuses on /igh/ and /ur/ and is a Blue level 4 book band.

Can you sort all the words on this page into two groups?

Fur

Right

Light

Words with **igh**

Turn

Surf

Sight

Might

Words with **ur**

Burn

Curb

Night

They are off on a trip. They must get a flight at midnight.

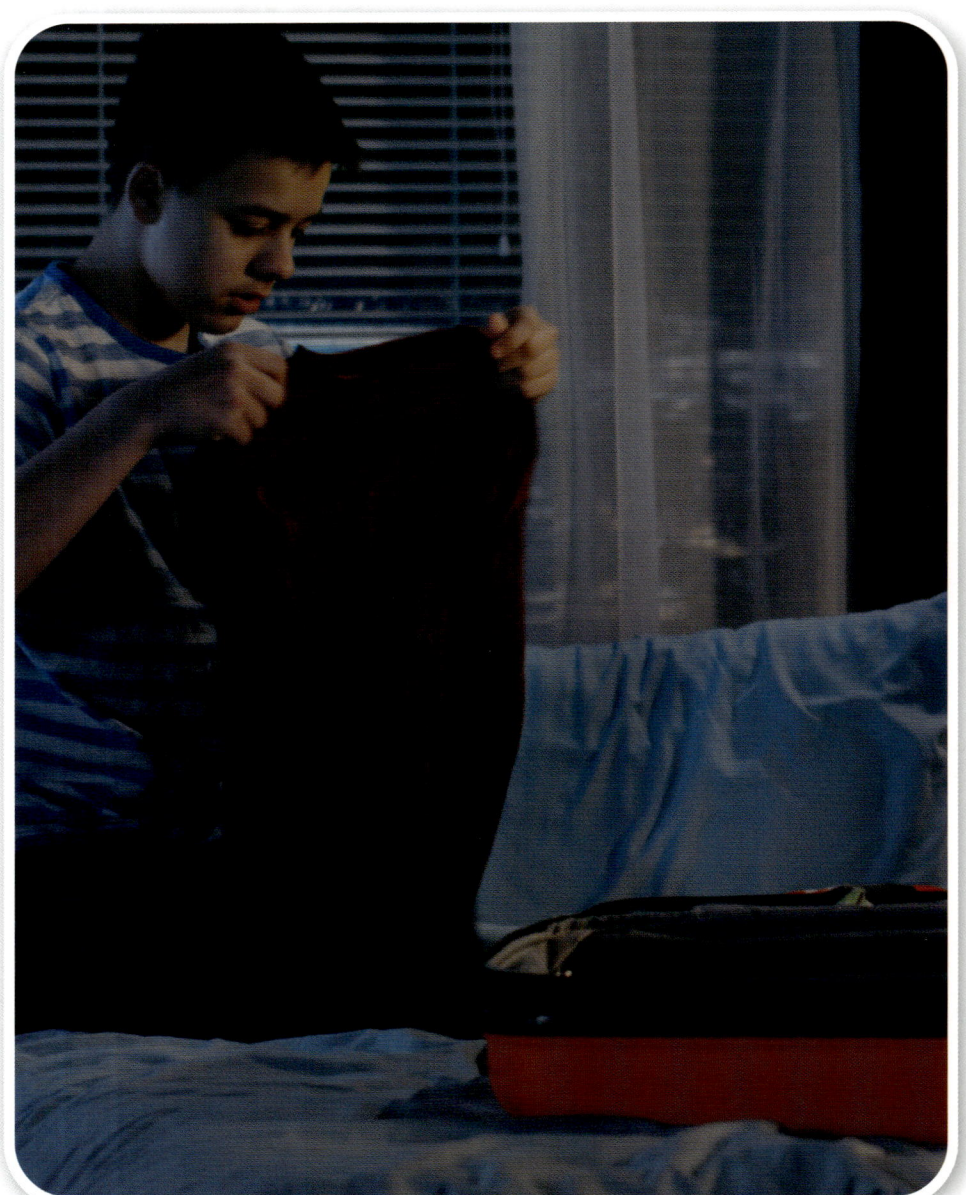

They will need to rush. They might miss the flight. They must rush to the van.

They need to get the bags in the back of the van.

They will need to go in the van to get to the jet.

They look for a spot to park the van.
They look left and right.

They park the van next to the curb. Then they get the bags out.

They must find the check-in desk.
They can turn the bags in there.

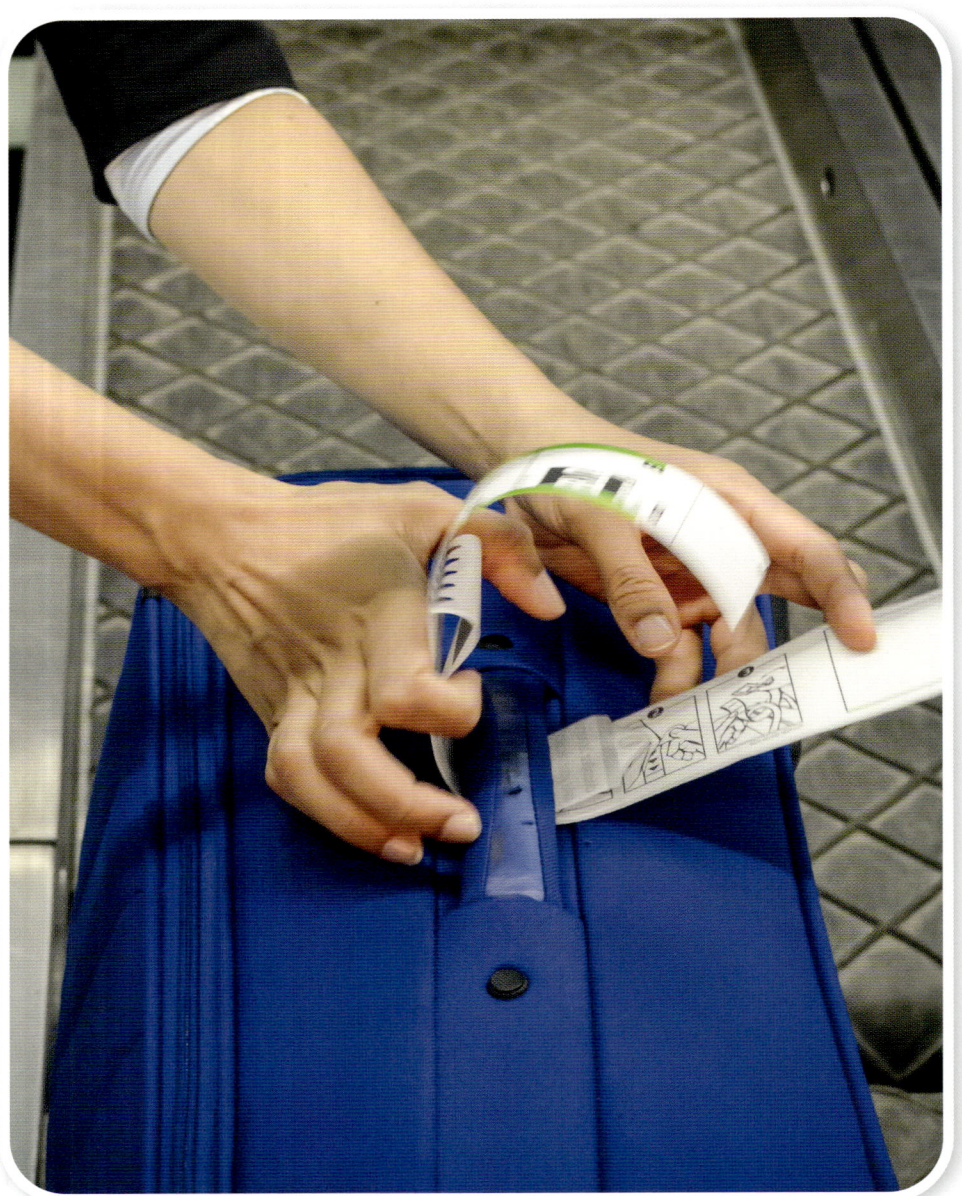

It is midnight. Now they must get on the jet.

The jet starts up. They feel a lurch as it turns right.

There is a big woosh as the jet sets off from the tarmac.

The jet is up high. They can see lots of lights at night.

The flight will be long. They all curl up and have a nap.

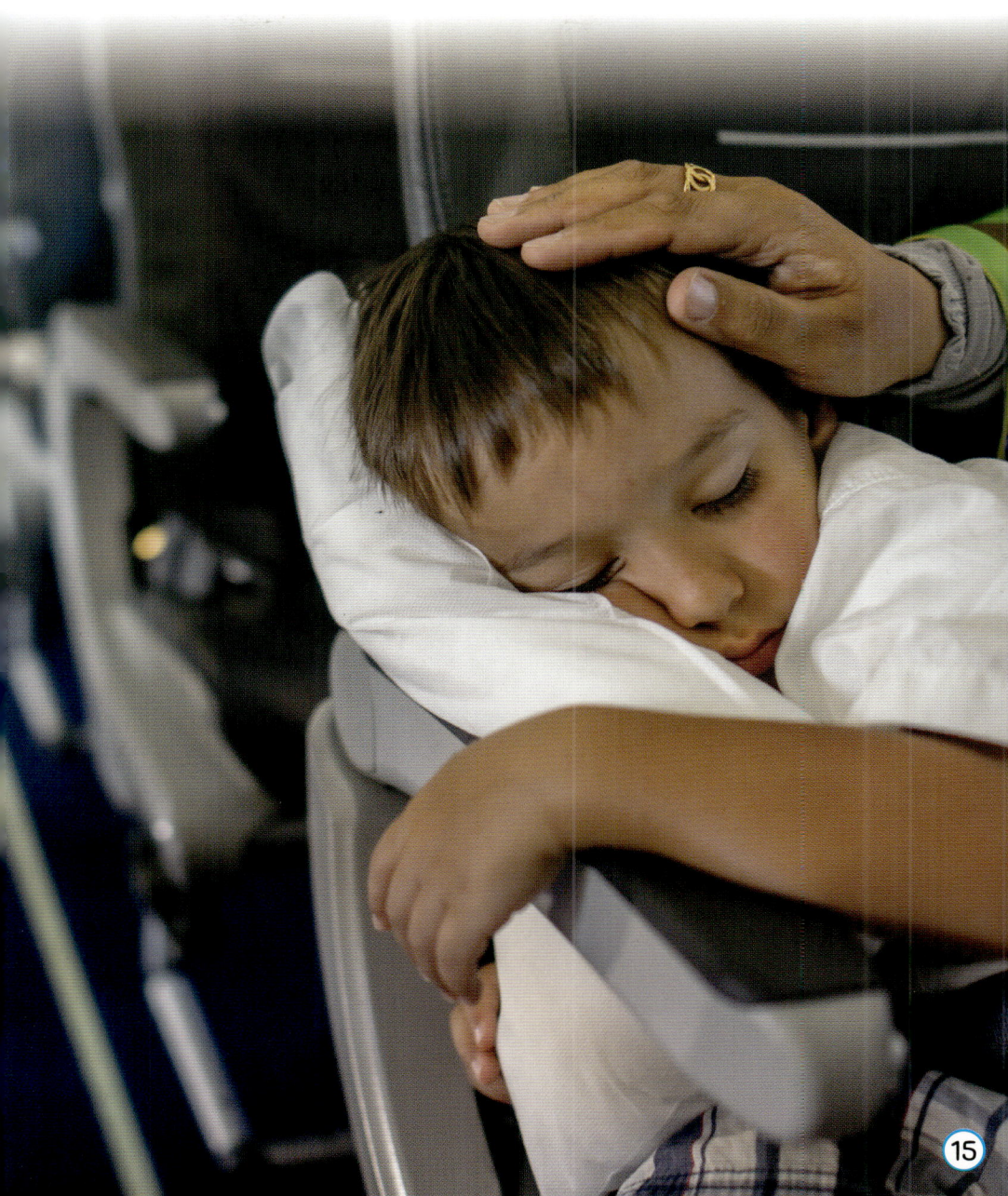

©2023 **BookLife Publishing Ltd.**
King's Lynn, Norfolk, PE30 4LS, UK.

ISBN 978-1-80505-053-7

All rights reserved. Printed in China.
A catalogue record for this book is
available from the British Library.

Night Flight
Written by Charis Mather
Designed by Jasmine Pointer

An Introduction to BookLife Readers...

Our Readers have been specifically created in line with the London Institute of Education's approach to book banding and are phonetically decodable and ordered to support each phase of Letters and Sounds.

Each book has been created to provide the best possible reading and learning experience. Our aim is to share our love of books with children, providing both emerging readers and prolific page-turners with beautiful books that are guaranteed to provoke interest and learning, regardless of ability.

BOOK BAND GRADED using the Institute of Education's approach to levelling.

PHONETICALLY DECODABLE supporting each phase of Letters and Sounds.

EXERCISES AND QUESTIONS to offer reinforcement and to ascertain comprehension.

CLEAR DESIGN to inspire and provoke engagement, providing the reader with clear visual representations of each non-fiction topic.

AUTHOR INSIGHT:
CHARIS MATHER

Charis Mather is a children's author at BookLife Publishing who has a love for reading and writing. Her studies in linguistics and experiences working with young readers have given her a knack for writing material that suits a range of ages and skill levels. Charis is passionate about producing books that emphasise the fun in reading and is convinced that no matter how much you already know, there is always something new to learn.

PHASE 4
/igh/
/ur/

This book focuses on /igh/ and /ur/ and is a Blue level 4 book band.

Image Credits Images are courtesy of Shutterstock.com. With thanks to Getty Images, Thinkstock Photo and iStockphoto. Cover – Sanit Fuangnakhon, CNGVahid, Little_Monster_2070. Suprun Vitaly. 4–5 – Frame Stock Footage, David Pereiras. 6–7 – Quisquilia, Kichigin. 8–9 – Jack Frog, Jens Goepfert. 10–11 – sebastianosecondi, Ilya Osovetskiy. 12–13 – Guido Benedetto, Leonardo da. 14–15 – Deyan Georgiev, Zurijeta.